Family Scrapbook

Toys and Fun
in the 1940s and 50s

Family Scrapbook

Toys and Fun
in the 1940s and 50s

Faye Gardner with Sue Dowell

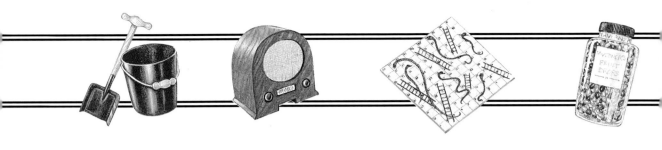

Family Scrapbook: **Toys and Fun in the 1940s and 50s**

Published by Evans Brothers Ltd in 2006
2A Portman Mansions
Chiltern St
London W1U 6NR

British Cataloguing in Publication Data
Gardner, Faye
Having Fun in Grandma's Day
3. Recreation - Great Britain - History - Juvenile literature
4. Great Britain - Social life and customs - 20th century - Juvenile literature
I, Title II Dowell, Sue
790'. 0941'09044

ISBN 0 237 52906 8
13 digit ISBN (from 1 January 2007) 978 0 237 52906 2

Acknowledgements
Planning and production by Discovery Books Limited
Edited by Faye Gardner
Designed by Ian Winton
Commissioned photography by Alex Ramsay
Illustrations by Stuart Lafford
First published in 1997. This edition published by Evans Brothers in 2006

For permission to reproduce copyright material, the author and publisher gratefully acknowledge the following:
The Advertising Archive Limited: 13, 15 (bottom); Aquarius Library: 17 (top); © BBC: 25 (top);
The Hulton Getty Picture Collection Limited: 10, 12 (bottom), 27 (bottom); Last Resort Picture Library: cover
(bottom left), 8, 24 (top), 25 (bottom), 27 (top) The London Borough of Richmond Upon Thames Local Studies
Collection: cover (bottom right), 7 (top), 26; Mary Evans Picture Library: 14; The National Motor Museum,
Beaulieu: 20; New Forest Ninth Centenary Trust: 21 (bottom); Peter Aphramian: 16; Radio Times: 24 (bottom);
The Robert Opie Collection: 17 (bottom); Science and Society Picture Library: 18;
Topham Picturepoint: 11 (top), 15 (top), 22. © Evans Brothers Limited 1997

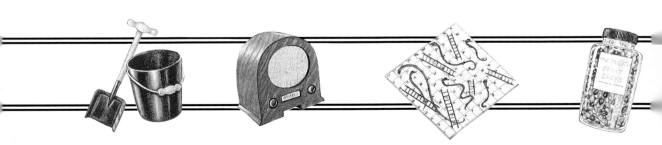

CONTENTS

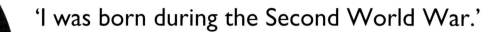

'I was born during the Second World War.'

My name is Sue and I am a grandmother. I have one granddaughter, Amy, who is five years old.

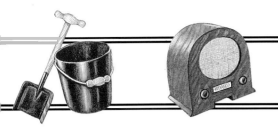

When I was young, I lived at Number 9 Palmerston Road, in Twickenham, which is near London. In the picture on the right you can see how Twickenham looked then.

My dad was a fireman and my mum was a housewife. I had two older brothers and a cousin to play with. The picture on the left shows us outside our house.

I was born in 1942, during the Second World War. Life was much harder just after the war than it is now. Many things were in short supply, but we still managed to have fun. I am going to tell you about some of the things we did.

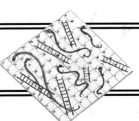

'There was no TV.'

Our house was very small so we were not allowed to play indoors unless it was raining. When I was young there was no TV in the house and no video games or computers to play with.

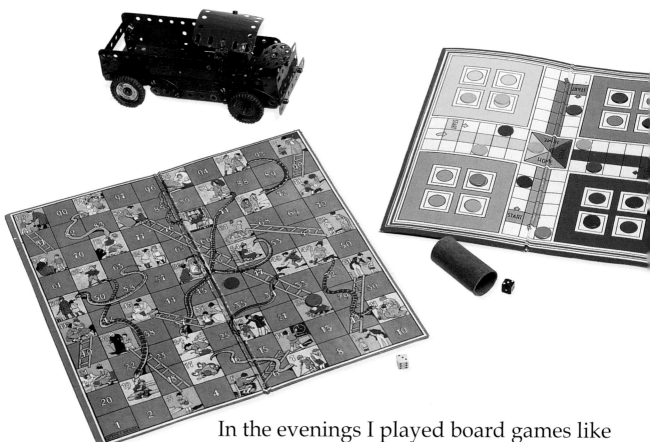

In the evenings I played board games like snakes and ladders or ludo with my brothers. Sometimes they would let me make things out of their Meccano set.

We were only given new toys for our birthday or for Christmas. One year my brother Roddy got a boat and I got a doll's cot and a teddy bear.

My dad made most of our toys himself. He made this crane for my brother Fred.

'We played on the bomb sites.'

Many streets were bombed during the war so there were always lots of exciting places to play. My brothers liked to play on the **bomb sites** with their friends.

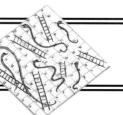

We also played hopscotch and marbles on the pavement outside our house. Sometimes we dressed up as soldiers and nurses.

I spent a lot of time skipping in the back yard, but my favourite game was five stones. You had to put five small stones on to the back of your hand. Then you tossed them in the air, turned your hand over and caught as many as you could.

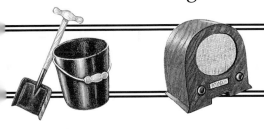
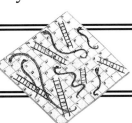

'I got sixpence pocket money.'

Every Saturday I was given sixpence pocket-money. That's six old pence, not 6p that we use today. This is what the old money used to look like.

Threepence

Two shillings and sixpence

Penny

Ha'penny

Sixpence

Two shillings

Farthing

Shilling

Sixpence was worth about 3p in today's money. That might not seem very much but you could buy a lot more for 3p when I was young than you can today.

I used to spend some of my money on
sweets. A stick of toffee cost about 2 1/2 old pence (about 1p).
Mars bars were my favourite sweet. They cost threepence
ha'penny (3 1/2 old pence or less than 2p).

'Books were too expensive.'

I loved reading but books were too expensive. I used to borrow them from the library. There was a separate section for children. My favourite books were the *St Clare's* and *Famous Five* stories by Enid Blyton.

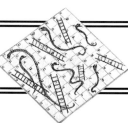

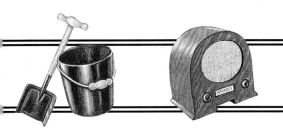

We also liked to read comics. They were full of funny stories, cartoons and jokes. When we were young we read *Dandy* or *Beano*. They cost two pence each (less than 1p). When I got older I read *Eagle* or *School Friend*.

During the war there was a shortage of paper. The comics did not have many pages inside and you could only buy them once a **fortnight**.

'Cinemas were like palaces.'

There were three cinemas in Twickenham and they were always busy. They were called the Odeon, the Regal and the Gaumont. The cinemas were much bigger and grander inside than they are today. They were like palaces.

It cost sixpence (3p) to sit downstairs and ninepence (4p) to sit upstairs. I liked the action films the best. My favourite film was called *Tarzan and the Amazons*.

Sometimes our parents would give us enough money to buy an ice cream. We didn't have much choice: we could either have a tub with a little wooden spoon, or a choc ice.

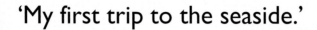
'My first trip to the seaside.'

When I was five years old I had my first trip to the seaside. We went with some of our neighbours to Exmouth in Devon.

My dad **hired** a car and our friends went by steam train.

COME TO
EXMOUTH
IN SUNNY SOUTH DEVON
for your holidays

ILLUSTRATED GUIDE
and all information from
Miss BROWN, Information Bureau
EXMOUTH

TRAVEL "SOUTHERN" RAILWAY · Restaurant Car Express from London (Waterloo)
THROUGH L M S TRAINS FROM MIDLANDS AND NORTH

We stayed in a small **bungalow** right by the sea.

People wore different clothes on the beach in those days. Some men just wore the same jackets and trousers that they wore every day. Most of them wore caps. My dad wore long shorts instead of trunks.

Mum's swimming costume was made of wool and had a little belt. It must have been very itchy!

I didn't have a swimming costume at all so I went into the sea in my knickers!

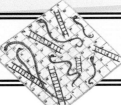

'Most city children never saw the countryside.'

Few families had cars when I was young. They were just too expensive. Petrol was in short supply after the war, too. People didn't travel around as much as they do today. Most city children never saw the countryside.

We were lucky. When I was ten, my dad saved enough money to buy our first car. It was a grey Ford Anglia and it looked like this.

FDL 968

Mum and Dad used to take us out for picnics in the countryside on Sunday afternoons.

Once a year we visited our cousins who lived in a cottage in the New Forest.

We used to play outside in the woods and walk to the beach to swim in the sea.

'The coronation was a special day.'

In 1953 the present Queen Elizabeth was crowned at Westminster Abbey in London.

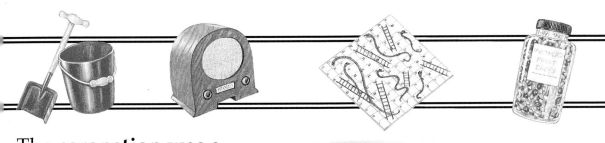

The **coronation** was a really special day for everyone. There were parties in the streets and everybody was happy. Every school child was given a **souvenir**. I got a coronation mug.

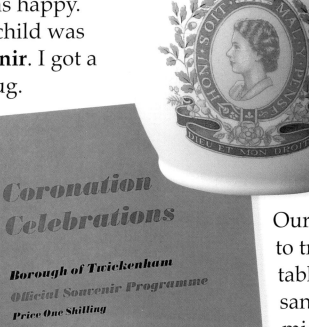

Coronation Celebrations

Borough of Twickenham

Official Souvenir Programme

Price One Shilling

Our street was closed to traffic. People put tables of cakes and sandwiches in the middle of the road and we hung coloured flags on the lampposts. Even the **mayor** joined in the fun.

We **hired** a TV set for the day just to watch the **ceremony**. My dad turned his garage into a bar and in the evening everyone went to a firework display in the nearby rugby ground.

'Everyone listened to the wireless.'

Although there were few TVs around, everyone listened to the **wireless**. Wireless sets were much bigger then than they are today. They always took about a minute to warm up.

We used to listen to radio programmes together in the evenings. There were lots of special programmes for children.

My favourite was *Life with the Lions*. My brothers liked the space programme *Journey into Space* and a detective series called *Dick Barton, Special Agent*. In the picture above you can see some actors recording a *Dick Barton* programme in the studio.

When I was 13 we bought our first TV set. It was a big, heavy machine with a small screen. There was just one channel and it only showed programmes in the evenings. The pictures were black and white and many of the programmes were news or **documentaries** about the war. I preferred listening to the wireless.

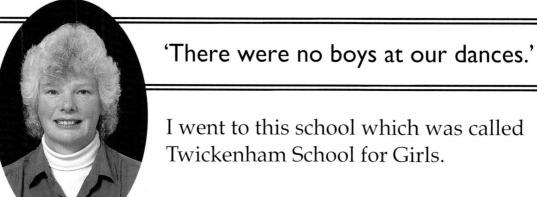

'There were no boys at our dances.'

I went to this school which was called Twickenham School for Girls.

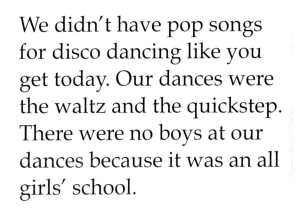

Sometimes we used to have school parties called 'socials'. We all brought records from home to dance to.

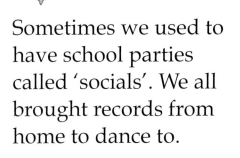

We didn't have pop songs for disco dancing like you get today. Our dances were the waltz and the quickstep. There were no boys at our dances because it was an all girls' school.

Once we wore paper petticoats under our skirts to make them look like proper dance skirts. Our headmistress told us off because they showed our thighs when we danced. We were not allowed to wear them again!

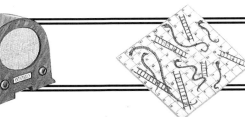

'We had good times then.'

Having fun was very different when I was young from what it is today. We often had to make our own games and toys, but I expect we enjoyed ourselves just as much as you do.

We had good times then.

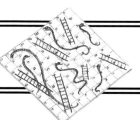

GLOSSARY

Bomb site A place that has been destroyed by bombs.

Bungalow A single-storey house.

Ceremony An event to mark a special occasion.

Coronation A ceremony in which someone is crowned king or queen.

Documentary A programme about real life, not a made-up story.

Fortnight Two weeks.

Hire To pay money to borrow something.

Mayor A person who is in charge of a town or city.

Souvenir A thing you keep to remind you of something that happened in the past.

Wireless A radio.

OTHER BOOKS TO READ

Other books about twentieth-century history for younger readers published by Evans include:

Rainbows *When Grandma Was Young*
Rainbows *When Dad Was Young*
Rainbows *What Was It Like Before Television?*
Tell Me About *Emmeline Pankhurst*
Tell Me About *Enid Blyton*

Britain Through The Ages *Britain Since 1930*
Alpha *1960s*
Take Ten Years *1930s, 1940s, 1950s, 1960s, 1970s, 1980s*

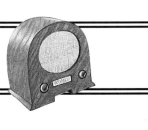
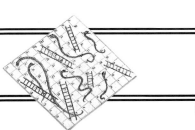

INDEX

The publishers would like to thank Susan Dowell and Heather Batt and family for their help in the preparation of this book. The publishers would also like to thank Mr F G Lane for kind permission to use his photographs: cover (right), back cover, title page, 7 (bottom), 9, 11 (bottom), 19, 21, 28.

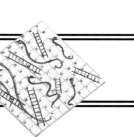